WILD & FRI

A COOKBOOK AND GUIDE TO NORTHWEST BLACKBERRIES

Written and Compiled By Kaethe Fulton

Illustrations By Erika Norwood

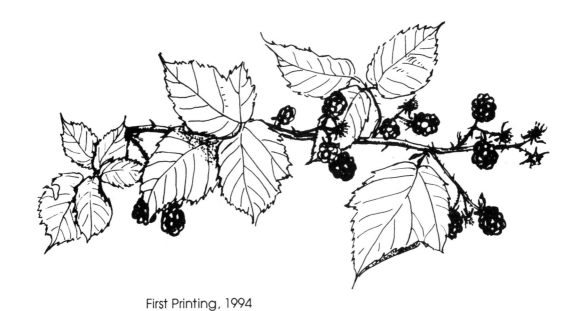

First Printing, 1994

Kaethe Fulton
Grace & Loie
11213 N.E. 141st Street
Kirkland, WA   98034
206-488-6927

TABLE OF CONTENTS

FORWARD

"The honey-feast of the berries has stunned them;
they believe in heaven."   - Plath

A Native American legend tells of a time when the blackberry was pale, with no luster and little flavor. In the days when Indians gathered these berries, there lived an Indian Princess who loved a brave young hunter. Unfortunately, to increase her tribe's strength in time of war, as an infant, she had been promised in marriage to the old Chief of a neighboring tribe. Years passed, and the marriage took place as planned. According to custom, symbolic offerings of food were brought to the wedding. Bitter at having his love for the Princess thwarted, the young hunter brought only the wild blackberries which were not particularly prized by the Indians. But, when the Princess looked into the hunter's cedar basket, the color of the berries became rich and deep, their aroma sweet, their flavor delicious. The love which shone in the faces of the young lovers was reflected in the brightness of the berries. "What a rare gift you have brought", she said. To this day, the wild blackberry has maintained the rich color and sweet goodness of the wedding day.

I was first introduced to the wild blackberries of the Northwest when I moved to Washington from Colorado. I lived in a small beach cabin with my two dogs. We moved in during an early spring storm, when the weather cleared it stayed warm and sunny. By early summer our cabin was surrounded by wild Himalayan Blackberry vines. I was amazed, and I too thought it was a rare gift. I also thought it was a sign from God; a sign that my impulsive move to Washington had been the right move, and that my life would be full here; as full as the blackberry vines surrounding my cabin.

I started to pick blackberries and make pies and cobblers. When I ran out of recipes, I asked my neighbors for some of their favorites. I put ads in newspapers asking others to send me recipes, too. I decided to write a cookbook and share all the recipes I gathered.

I am grateful to all who responded to my requests. I am very grateful to Erika Norwood, and her family, who tested recipes. She also added a few of her own. Her illustrations bring the recipes and text to life. Her support has made this effort possible, as has the support and assistance of my husband Jon, Lisa Olsen, Chris and Jeff Fulton, and Dorothy and Stan Stapp. Thank you all.

I will update and revise this edition in the future. If you have a favorite recipe you would like to share with others, please send it to me for consideration for my next edition.

I hope this cookbook and guide will help you to enjoy the natural bounty of the blackberries of the northwest, they're wild and free.

Kaethe Fulton

INTRODUCTION

"It's a nice way to live,
Just taking what Nature is willing to give,
Not forcing her hand with harrow or plow."   - Robert Frost

Many of the best things in life are free. Wild blackberries, which occur abundantly in the Northwest, are a perfect example. Throughout the mid to late summer months they seem to be everywhere wild, and free for the picking. They are important to humans and wildlife. Blackberries are a source of food for all, the vines a source of shelter. Together they are the perfect place to find food, build a nest or hide from a predator. They also have a medicinal use.

The blackberry vine has long been recognized as a valuable plant with healing properties. Herodotus believed that blackberry plants cured gout. A tenth century treatise on plants, The Leechbook of Bald, recommended pounded blackberry leaves placed over the heart as a cure for heartache. Tudor herbalists mixed blackberry juice with honey and wine as a cure for passions of the heart. In early American medicine, blackberry-root extract was a main ingredient in a seventeenth-century cholera remedy and blackberry leaves were considered a cure for diabetes. Even today, a cup of blackberry tea is used by some as a cure for diarrhea.

Blackberry picking has a place in history, too. For many, it is, and has been, an important rite of summer. While researching this book, I received many letters from people with fond memories of family blackberry picking outings. It seemed everyone enjoyed the day and the fruits of the day's labor, even the family dog. Many people described a favorite blackberry patch they like to return to year after year.

Estimates from experts on the number of berry species which occur in the United States vary widely, anywhere from 50 to 390 species. Hitchcock and Cronquist, authors of the definitive work on the plantlife of the Northwest, Flora of the Pacific Northwest , document over twenty species of the Rubus (brambleberries, blackberries and raspberries) genus of the Rosaceae (Rose) family occurring in the Northwest region alone. Hitchcock and Cronquist document three species as being most abundant. My research and wanderings concur. These three species, Trailing Blackberry, Evergreen Blackberry, and Himalayan Blackberry will be the focus of this book. They can be used interchangeably in the recipes included.

For the purpose of this book, Northwest is defined as including Washington, Oregon, Northern California, Idaho, Southern British Columbia and Western Montana. Not all areas of this region are home to wild blackberries, but many will be. Blackberries can be found most commonly in recently disturbed landscapes; urban, suburban and rural. Look for blackberries in burned, logged, and cleared areas, the sites of recent development, neighborhood parks, vacant lots, along fences and roadways, in pastures, and even your own backyard. Blackberries can be found in open fields and in dense woodlands, from coastal areas to mid-montane.

Blackberries grow best in well drained soils, with partial shade. The thick cane stems can occur upright and arching, forming brambles and as long, trailing vines. The blossoms of blackberry plants resemble small wild roses.

When cooking with wild berries it should be kept in mind that there are no guarantees. Sugar and acid content can vary from plant to plant, from year to year. Conditions depend on the soil content, amount of sunshine and rainfall, the temperature and even the number of bees in the area. Blackberries are self-pollinating, but the number of berries can be reduced by as much as 50% if there are few bees in the area. The amount of rain a blackberry plant receives one year can affect the number of berries produced the next. It has been noted that the more water a plant receives in August, the more berries will be produced the next year.

As members of the Rosaceae family, blackberries are related to apples, pears, cherries, strawberries, rosehips, spirea and mountain ash, among many others. Along with other members of this family, blackberries are an excellent source of vitamins. A cup of blackberries can provide 30 milligrams of Vitamin C, 290 International Units of Vitamin A, 46 milligrams of Calcium, 240 milligrams of Potassium, small amounts of other vitamins and minerals and, about 95 calories.

This book will focus on the characteristics of the three most common species of blackberries found in the Northwest. It will also include tips on picking and storage, a collection of recipes, and additional pages for noting favorite blackberry patch locations and new recipes.

IDENTIFICATION OF THREE SPECIES OF BLACKBERRIES COMMONLY FOUND IN THE NORTHWEST

Trailing Blackberry (Rubus ursinus)

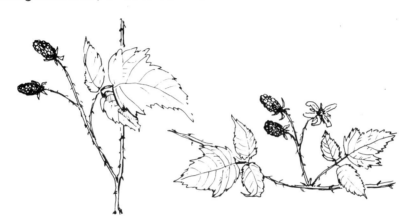

The Trailing Blackberry is the Northwest's only native blackberry. It is known by a variety of names, including Pacific Dewberry, Dewberry and Douglasberry (R. macropetalus, R. vitifolius, R. helleri).

Hitchcock and Cronquist note that the stems are slender, occur in a trailing configuration, rather than as a shrub or bush. The stems are armed with slender thorns and slightly flattened prickles. The leaves are trifoliate, occurring in three's. The plants are dioecious, occurring as either male or female, both having white flowers. The plants can be distinguished from each other because the male plant flowers are larger (can be up to twice the size) than the female plant flowers. It is the female plant alone which produces the berries.

As the only native blackberry species, Trailing Blackberries are more cold sensitive, and tend to ripen earlier than other blackberry species found in the region. Look for them in mid-summer (July), at the same time the Fireweed begins to bloom. The berries can be smaller and more oblong in shape than those of the other species, and while not as naturally sweet, they do taste great right off the vine. They are the best blackberry to use in pies as the sugar and baking enhance their flavor.

Evergreen Blackberry (Rubus laciniatus)

Evergreen Blackberries are a European species which was introduced into the Northwest. They are easily distinguished from other species by their thick reddish stems and their distinctive lobed and pointed leaves. (Evergreen blackberries are also known as the Cut-leaf Blackberry.) The leaves occur in sets of five. A close examination of a leaf will show both the top and bottom surfaces to be green, with the bottom surface containing many hairs. The plants are monoecious, with both sexes occurring on the same plant. The flowers range in color from white to pinkish white. The plants are armed with thorns (larger than those on the Trailing Blackberry) with large and often flattened prickles.

Evergreen Blackberries ripen in late-August to September. They can be small or large, and sweet. (As was noted earlier, growing conditions have a great deal to do with the size and sweetness of the berries.) They are firm enough to maintain their shape in pies and other dishes. The seed can seem coarse or bony. Like the Trailing Blackberry, Evergreen Blackberries are highly prized by blackberry pickers.

Himalayan Blackberry (Rubus discolor)

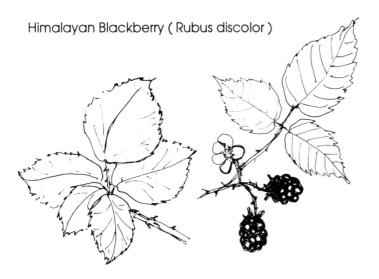

The Himalayan Blackberry is the most abundant, almost ubiquitous, specie in the region. It is an old world plant, introduced into the Northwest, and doing very well in it's new home. The leaves are larger than those of other species, are coarsely toothed, and occur in sets of three or five. A close inspection of the leaf surfaces will find the top green and the bottom whitish. The stems are thick, woody and stout, and the plants are armed with large thorns and hooked prickles. The plants are monoecious, with both sexes occurring on the same plant. The flowers range in color from white to pinkish and they bloom in profusion.

The Himalayan Blackberry is large in size and deep in color and flavor. Along with the Evergreen Blackberry, the Himalayan ripens from mid-August to late September, and can often be found into October.

SIDE BY SIDE LEAF COMPARISONS FOR QUICK IDENTIFICATION

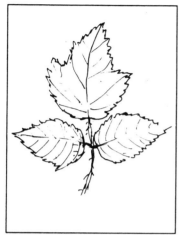

Trailing Blackberry

Evergreen Blackberry

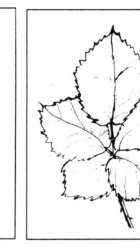

Himalayan Blackberry

ANATOMY OF A BLACKBERRY

Stem

Drupelet - Each contains a seed.

TIPS ON PICKING BLACKBERRIES

"Picking wild berries is the sweetest and best of our
             vagrant summer pleasures." - Jager

Berry picking may well be one of the sweetest and best summertime pleasures. For many, it is a favorite summertime activity. Berry picking has much more to offer than just delicious berries. It is a chance to gather our own food, and fully enjoy both the warmth and fruits of the season. Berry picking is an experience filled with fresh air, exercise, the songs of birds, encounters with wildlife and more. But be warned, you may also experience bug bites, scratches, stains and torn clothes. If it is raining you'll get wet and if it is warm and sunny you will get hot. Berry picking is an activity long remembered and cherished. My advice is to be prepared with the dreams of favorite blackberry dishes.

You should also never underestimate the importance of the right equipment in a berry picking outing. It will increase your pleasure and your take. Plan to wear long sleeves, long pants, sturdy shoes, and a hat to provide some shade. Some berry pickers choose to wear gloves with the fingers cut off to provide even greater protection from thorns; you might want to consider them too. The long thorny vines have both foot-catching and thorn-sticking abilities, be alert. Your pail should be light and shallow. The bottom half of a milk carton or a plastic container with strings attached to tie around your neck, is ideal. This leaves your hands free to pick and your collection point near. A shallow pail will keep too many berries from being crushed by the weight of other berries. Also bring one large container, a box bottom or oblong pan, to empty smaller pails into as they fill. A type of hook, even a slightly straightened coathanger will come in handy for grabbing those out of reach, full of berries, vines.

Time of day is important, too. On a sunny day, get out early and look for berries in the morning sun. It will be cooler than later in the day and some berry pickers feel that blackberries picked in the morning are sweeter and last longer than those picked in the afternoon.

Blackberries are ripest and sweetest when they lose their shine and begin to look dull. A ripe blackberry will easily leave the stem, almost falling into your hand. Do not try to force a blackberry off the vine, those which do not leave the stem easily will be sour. When picked, the blackberry core remains with the berry. (This is distinctly different from the raspberry, whose core remains on the stem when picked.)

Pick the entire bramble or vine of ripe berries before moving on to another. Then skip a few to leave berries for others. Watch out for young plants and try not to trample long vines in your search for berries.

After a successful berry picking adventure, your next concern is how to enjoy them, now and throughout the year.

STORING BLACKBERRIES

"I've picked a pail of blackberries. What do I do with
them now?"   - Kaethe Barton, 1986

Once picked, blackberries should be used as soon as possible, or stored for future use. If possible, plan to use fresh berries within three to four hours of picking. If you will be serving them fresh, later in the day, just store them in the refrigerator, right off the vine. It is not necessary to clean them before refrigeration. Those not used immediately can be frozen or canned, either process will leave them perfectly good for the recipes included here.

To clean the berries just pick out any stems, leaves and bugs. Wash them by placing the berries in a colander and rinsing, allow them to drain immediately.

To prepare blackberries for freezing, rinse and drain. For loose-packed storage, spread a layer of blackberries on a cookie sheet and freeze them until they are very hard. Place the frozen berries in freezer bags, eliminate all air, and seal the bag. The berries can be stored in a freezer for as long as one year. Crushed berries can also be frozen for one year in containers. Be sure to leave 1/2 inch of space at the top of the container for expansion. Freeze crushed berries in containers which are the right size for a particular recipe, such as enough berries to make one cobbler or pie.

Blackberries can also be frozen with sugar or in a sugar syrup. To freeze with sugar, add 1/2 cup of superfine sugar for every 4 cups of berries and mix the sugar and berries gently together. To freeze blackberries in a sugar syrup, boil 3/4 cup sugar with 1 cup water, for each 4 cups of blackberries. Cool the syrup mixture then pour it over the berries in freezer containers. Leave 1/2 inch for expansion, seal the containers and freeze. The berries will be good for one year.

Blackberries can be canned for use at other times of the year. Prepare a syrup using four cups water and three cups sugar, bring the mixture to a boil in a medium saucepan. (This makes enough syrup for eight pint jars.) Pack fresh blackberries in hot canning jars. Pour the syrup into the jars, leaving 1/2 inch at the top, and seal the jars. Boil the jars in a boiling water bath for fifteen minutes for pint and twenty minutes for quart jars.

RECIPES

The recipes included are a compilation of those donated in response to my requests and personal variations of popular recipes which have been adapted over the years.

When preparing these recipes, please keep in mind that blackberries can be pleasingly combined with other members of the Rosaceae family. Lemons and limes are also good compliments to blackberries.

Blackberries can be substituted in these recipes by other brambleberries, such as loganberries, marionberries and boysenberries.

Blank pages have been included to provide space for favorite recipes not a part of this collection. I hope you will consider sharing your family favorites with me to be included in my next edition. Please send recipes and/or comments to Kaethe Fulton at Grace & Loie, 11213 N.E. 141st St. Kirkland, WA 98034.

BEVERAGES

Blackberry Juice

For jelly and jam recipes:

Pick 2 1/2 - 3 quarts blackberries, combining 75% ripe berries with 25% under ripe berries. Sort and wash, removing any stems. Crush berries in a pot. Add 3/4 cup water, cover and bring to a boil over high heat. Reduce heat and simmer for 5 minutes. Put blackberry mixture into a damp jelly bag or into a colander lined with muslin, to extract the juice.

The clearest juice comes from juices that have dripped through the bag without being pressed.

A greater yield of juice will be obtained by twisting the jelly bag or muslin, and squeezing the juice through.

For Blackberry juice to use in beverages:

Use only ripe blackberries and add 1/2 cup water.

Blackberry Drink

Milk	1 cup
Blackberries	1/4 cup
Honey or Sugar	To taste

Blend ingredients in a blender on medium speed.
Makes one drink.

A. Louise Cooper
Woodinville, WA.

Blackberry Fruit Drink

Ripe Blackberries
Vinegar

Fill jars (any size, any number) with ripe blackberries; fill spaces between berries with vinegar and let stand for one month. Strain off the juices, serve sweetened with sugar and diluted with iced water.

Store extra juice in sterilized containers.

Mary Lou Muth
Auburn, WA.

Blackberry Milkshake

Blackberries	1 cup
Vanilla Ice Cream	1 1/2 cups
Milk	1/4 - 1/2 cup
Nutmeg	dash
Crunchy Peanut Butter	1 Tbsp.(optional)

Put all ingredients in a blender container and blend to desired thickness. (The longer blended, the thinner the milkshake becomes. If too thin, store in freezer until desired thickness is reached.)

Makes approximately 3 cups.

Adrianne J. Flint
Lynnwood, WA

Blackberry Punch

Blackberry Juice	2 - 4 cups
Frozen Lemon Juice	1/2 - 1 can
7-Up	To taste
Sugar	To taste

Combine blackberry juice, lemon juice, 7-Up and sugar in a large bowl.

Marian Tague
Indianola, WA

Curative Blackberry Tea

Blackberry Root   dried and crushed
Blackberry Leaves   dried
Boiling Water

Cover a tsp. of blackberry root and/or leaves with water.
Let steep several minutes before drinking.

One or two cups of Blackberry tea are considered a cure
for diarrhea. Eating fresh berries works well too.

Jannell O. Church
Spanaway, WA

Blackberry Ice Cubes for Lemonade

Blackberries   2 cups
Sugar   1/2 cup
Cold Water   1 cup

Press berries through sieve. Pour cold water through sieve
into pressed berries. Stir in sugar and freeze mixture into
ice cubes. Serve in lemonade.

Makes two standard trays.

Jean Baker
Bothell, WA

Blackberry Brandy

Blackberries	2 1/2 cups
Sugar	1 1/2 cups
Brandy	2 cups

Crush blackberries and combine with 1 cup brandy in a glass jar. Cover tightly, shake and let stand for one week.

Strain mixture through cheesecloth to remove juice, then strain juice again. Add remaining 1 cup brandy and sugar. Let stand for two weeks before drinking. Store brandy in a cool dark place.

Blackberry Cordial

Blackberry Juice	1 quart
Sugar	4 cups
Mace	1/2 Tbsp.
Cinnamon	1 Tbsp.
Cloves	4 tsp.
French Brandy	1 pint

Combine all ingredients except the Brandy and boil together for 15 minutes. Cool and strain. To each quart of juice, add one pint of Brandy and bottle at once in liquor bottles. Cork and seal.

Makes 3 1/2 pints.

Jean Baker
Bothell, WA.

Non Alcoholic Blackberry Cordial

Blackberry Juice	1 Qt.
Sugar	2 cups
Grated Nutmeg	1/2 oz.
Cinnamon	1/4 oz. stick
Whole Cloves	1/4 oz.
Mace	small piece
Vanilla	4 Tbsp.

Mash and strain blackberries through cheesecloth, without heating them, to make 1 quart. Add spices tied in a bag. Boil juice with spice bag for 25 minutes, removing scum as it rises. Remove spice bag and add 4 Tbsp. vanilla. Pour into sterilized jars and seal.

Blackberry Liqueur

Ripe Blackberries	3 cups
Vodka	1 Fifth
Water	1 cup
Sugar	3 cups

Mix all ingredients in a wide-mouth glass container, taking care not to cut or crush the berries. Allow mixture to sit for 10 days. Pour mixture through a strainer or several thicknesses of cheesecloth and discard berries. (The berries can also be used as a topping for ice cream.) Pour liqueur into bottles and seal. (The liqueur may have a cloudy appearance.) Makes wonderful gifts.

Adrianne J. Flint's Blackberry Wine

Blackberries	**6 - 8 gallons**
Sugar	**5 + pounds**

Wash fresh blackberries and put into a large container. Mix in 5 pounds sugar and cover top with cloth, tied to keep out insects. Let mixture stand for 8 - 10 days.

Strain mixture through cheesecloth, squeezing the pulp so all juice is extracted. Measure juice. For each gallon of juice, add 1 1/2 pounds of sugar. Let mixture stand. When it stops foaming and bubbling, strain mixture, measure it again and again add 1 1/2 pounds of sugar for each gallon of juice. Let mixture stand until foaming and bubbling stops. Bottle wine.

Adrianne J. Flint
Lynnwood, WA

Mrs. Gadsdens's Blackberry Wine

Blackberries	**7 quarts**
Water	**5 1/2 quarts, divided**
White of 1 Egg	
Sugar	**7 pounds**

Mash blackberries, add 3 1/2 quarts of water and let stand for 24 hours. Strain mixture through thin cloth. In a separate container, beat egg white, add sugar and remaining water. Boil 5 minutes, skim and cool. Add the cooled sugar-water-egg mixture to the berries, stir well and place mixture in a jar. Skim and stir the mixture each morning for 10 days. Put mixture into a large jar or demijohn, cover with a clean cloth and let mixture stand until fermentation ceases. Siphon off wine and bottle.

Mrs. William Gadsden
Charleston, SC

Geannie Kuranko's Blackberry Wine

Blackberries	1 gallon
Lukewarm Water	1 gallon
Sugar	5 pounds, divided
Toasted Bread	2 pieces
Bread Baking Yeast	1 package

In a 5 gallon crock, crush berries and add water. Mix with wooden spoon and add 2 1/2 lbs. of sugar. Stir until dissolved. Float toasted bread on top of mixture and sprinkle toast with yeast. Cover crock with cheesecloth and let stand for 5 days. After 5 days, add remaining sugar and let stand, undisturbed, another 2 days. After 2 days, stir well and let stand for 3 weeks. After 3 weeks strain wine through cheesecloth to separate seeds. Siphon strained wine into a gallon jug. DO NOT CAP, but cover with a paper towel stuffed into neck of jug.

Geannie Kuranko
South Prairie, WA

BREADS & CAKES

Blackberry Bread or Cake

Flour	4 3/4 cups
Baking Powder	1 tsp.
Baking Soda	1 tsp.
Salt	1/2 tsp.
Butter	1 cup
Sugar	2 cups
Vanilla	1 tsp.
Eggs	4
Buttermilk	1 cup
Blackberries	2 cups
Powdered Sugar	1/2 cup

Combine flour, baking soda, baking powder and salt. In a mixing bowl cream butter with sugar and vanilla; beat until fluffy on medium speed. Add eggs, one at a time, beating well after each addition. Add dry ingredients and buttermilk alternately to beaten mixture, beating on low speed until just combined. Fold in blackberries and turn batter into a greased 10" fluted tube pan. Bake for 1 1/4 hour at 350°. May also be baked in two greased loaf pans for 40 minutes at 350° Dust with powdered sugar when cooled.

Serves: 12 - 14

Adrianne J. Flint   &   Mary McLaren
Lynwood, WA   Auburn, Wa.

Old English Blackberry Buns

Flour	1 1/8 cup
Baking Powder	1 tsp.
Salt	pinch
Butter	6 Tbsp.
Sugar	1/4 cup
Egg	1
Milk	approximately 2 Tbsp.
Blackberry Jam	as needed

Pre-heat oven to 375°

Sift together flour, baking powder and salt. Cut in butter and add sugar. Beat egg with milk. Make a well in the center of the flour mixture and add egg-milk mixture. Mix until forms a stiff dough.

Divide dough into balls the size of a walnut. Make a hole in the top of each and put a bit of blackberry jam in it. Pinch edges together and flatten lightly, place on a greased baking sheet. Brush each bun with milk, sprinkle with sugar and bake for 10 minutes at 375°. Reduce temperature to 350° and bake another 5 minutes.

June Long
Puyallup, WA.

Blackberry Coffee Cake

Flour	2 1/4 cups, divided
Sugar	1 cup
Baking Powder	2 tsp.
Salt	1 tsp.
Cinnamon	1/2 tsp.
Margarine	1/2 cup
Eggs	2
Vanilla	1 tsp.
Blackberries	3 1/2 cups
Brown Sugar	1/3 cup
Butter	2 Tbsp.
Pecans	1/2 cup, chopped

Pre-heat oven to 350°

In a large bowl, sift together 2 cups flour, sugar, baking powder, salt and cinnamon. Cut in margarine until mixture is crumbly. In another bowl, mix together eggs, milk and 1 c. vanilla. Pour egg mixture over flour mixture and mix until moistened. Spread batter into a greased 8" x 12" baking pan and distribute berries on top of the batter.

In a small bowl combine brown sugar, 1/4 cup flour and butter; mix with a fork until crumbly; add pecans and sprinkle mixture on top of cake. Bake for 45 minutes.

Mary McLaren
Auburn, WA

Blackberry Jam Cake

Sugar	1 1/2 cups
Butter	1 2/3 cup
Eggs	4, separated
Buttermilk	2/3 cup
Baking Soda	1 tsp.
Flour	2 cups, sifted
Cinnamon	1 tsp.
Allspice	1 tsp.
Cloves	1 tsp.
Blackberry Jam	1 cup

Cream together butter and sugar. Beat egg yolks and add to butter-sugar mixture. Add baking soda to buttermilk and add to mixture. Sift flour with spices and sift into mixture. Add jam and mix well. Beat egg whites until stiff and fold into batter. Pour mixture into three 8" pans that have been greased and lined with waxed paper. Bake for 30 minutes at 350°.
Top cake with your favorite icing.

Adrianne J. Flint
Lynwood, WA

Blackberry Jelly Roll

Eggs - room temperature	4
Baking Powder	1 tsp.
Salt	1/2 tsp.
Sugar	2/3 cup
Vanilla	1 tsp.
Cake flour	2/3 cup
Powdered sugar	As needed
Blackberry jam	1 cup
or cooked fresh blackberry filling	

Pre-heat oven to 400°.

Beat eggs with baking powder and salt, until thick and pale. Gradually beat in sugar and continue beating until very thick. Add vanilla. Sift the flour and fold into egg mixture.

Spread batter in a 10 x 15 inch jelly roll pan that has been greased, lined with waxed paper and greased again. Bake for 12 to 15 minutes until golden. Turn out on a towel sprinkled with powdered sugar. Peel off wax paper and roll up, enclosing in towel. Cool on a rack, and unroll when cool. Spread with jam and roll again, without towel.

Serves 10.

Blackberry Muffins

Unsalted Butter	1/2 cup (1 stick)
Eggs	2
Sugar	1 1/8 cups
Flour	3 cups, divided
Baking Powder	3 tsp.
Salt	1/2 tsp.
Baking Soda	pinch
Milk	1 cup
Vanilla	1 tsp.
Blackberries	2 cups

Pre-heat oven to 400°. Grease two - 12 cup muffin pans, or use liners.

In a large bowl cream butter with sugar and add eggs. Reserve 3 Tbs. of the flour, and combine the remaining flour with baking powder, salt and baking soda. Combine milk and vanilla. Alternately add the milk and flour mixture to the creamed butter and egg mixture. Sprinkle reserved flour over berries and gently fold berries into the mixture. Fill each muffin cup 3/4 full and sprinkle tops with sugar, if desired. Bake 15 - 20 minutes, until done.

Makes 18 - 24 muffins

Erika Norwood
Seattle, WA

Blackberry Rival Cake

Sugar	1 cup, heaping
Margarine	1/4 cup
Egg	1
Milk	1/2 cup
Flour	2 cups
Baking Powder	2 tsp.
Salt	1/2 tsp.
Blackberries	4 cups

Combine all ingredients except the berries and beat well. Gently stir in blackberries. Pour batter into a greased 9 x 13" pan. Make topping.

Topping:

Sugar	1/2 cup
Butter	1/4 cup
Cinnamon	1/2 tsp.

Melt butter and stir in sugar and cinnamon and spread this mixture on top of batter. Bake 45 minutes at 375° If using frozen berries, do not thaw them.

Blackberry Scones

Flour	2 cups, unsifted
Baking Powder	3 tsp.
Sugar	2 - 3 Tbsp.
Salt	1/2 tsp.
Butter	4 Tbsp.
Eggs	2, beaten
	(Reserve 1 Tbsp. of egg white for brushing on top of the scones.)
Cream	1/3 cup
Blackberries	3/4 - 1 cup

Combine flour, baking powder, sugar and salt in a bowl. Cut in butter until mixture is fine and crumbly. Beat eggs with cream and add to flour mixture. Turn dough out on floured board and knead a few times until dough is uniform. Divide dough into four parts. Roll or pat out each part to make a circle about 6 " in diameter. Scatter half of the blackberries on two of the circles. Top these two halves with the other two halves so the berries are sandwiched between the two halves of the scone dough. Brush the top circles with egg white and sprinkle with a little sugar, if desired. Cut each circle into four quarters and transfer to a baking sheet, about an inch apart. Bake at 400° for 15 minutes. Serve scones while warm.

Makes 8 scones.

Erika Norwood
Seattle, WA

Satsop Wild Blackberry Jam Squares

Flour	1 1/3 cups
Baking Soda	1/2 tsp.
Salt	1/2 tsp..
Light Brown Sugar	1 cup
Quick Cooking Oats	1/2 cup
Walnuts	1 cup, chopped
Butter	1 cup, melted
Raisins	1/4 cup, chopped
Wild Blackberry Jam	1/4 cup
Brandy	

Sift together flour, baking soda and salt. Add sugar, oats, walnuts and melted butter. Blend mixture well and press 1/2 mixture into well greased 7x11" pan.

Combine raisins and blackberry jam and spread over mixture in pan. Add remaining flour mixture carefully over jam layer. Bake at 375° for 30 minutes. Sprinkle with Brandy after removing from oven. Cut into squares, store in tin in freezer.

June Long
Puyallup, WA.

Wild Blackberry Squares

Crust:

Margarine	1 stick
Flour	1 1/2 cup
Sugar	2 Tbsp.

To make crust melt the margarine in the oven in a 13 x 9" pan. Add flour and sugar to melted margarine and mix with a fork and press mixture into bottom of pan with fingers.

Filling:

Sugar	1 - 1 1/2 cups
Flour	3/4 cup
Blackberries	4 cups
Cinnamon	1/2 tsp.

Mix together filling ingredients in bowl and spoon over crust.

Topping:

Sugar	1/2 cup
Flour	3/4 cup
Margarine	1/3 cup
Cinnamon	1/4 tsp.

Mix together topping ingredients and sprinkle over filling.

Bake for approximately 1 hour at 350°. Serve warm with cream or cold with whipped cream.

Queens Cake (Blackberry Torte)

Butter or Margarine	1/2 cup (1 cube)
Sugar	1/2 cup
Vanilla	1 tsp.
Eggs	2
Grated Lemon Peel	1 tsp.
Flour	2 cups
Potato flour or cornstarch	1/2 cup
Baking Soda	1 tsp.
Baking powder	1 tsp.

With electric mixer beat butter and sugar. Add eggs, vanilla and lemon peel. Combine flour, potato flour or cornstarch, baking soda and baking powder and add to above mixture. Press 2/3 of dough into well buttered and floured 8 inch Springform cake pan.

Fresh berry Filling:

Berries	2 cups
Sugar	3 Tbsp.
Tapioca	1 Tbsp.
Lemon juice	2 tsp.

Mix berries, sugar, tapioca and lemon juice, and pour over dough in pan. Make 1/2 inch round ropes from remaining dough, to make lattice over filling.

Bake at 350° degrees 20-30 minutes. Let cool 30 minutes, then run knife between cake and pan. Remove pan rim. Leave cake on bottom of pan. Sprinkle with powdered sugar.

Margie Albrecht
Seattle, Washington

Quick Upside Down Cake

Blackberries	5 cups
Sugar	1 cup
Blackberry or Lemon Jell-O	1 3oz. pkg.
Mini-marshmallows	3 cups
White or Yellow Cake Mix	1 pkg.

Grease well a 9x13x2" pan; sprinkle with jello and sugar. Top with marshmallows and berries. Cover with prepared cake batter. Bake at 350°for 50 minutes. Turn upside down on large plate or cookie sheet. Serve with dollop of whipped cream, or ice cream if you prefer.

Darlene Radke
Ferndale, WA

Wild Blackberry Cake

Eggs	2
Sugar	2 cups
Butter or Shortening	1/2 cup
Flour	2 1/2 cups
Salt	1 tsp.
Nutmeg	1/4 tsp.
Cinnamon	1/4 tsp.
Cloves	1/4 tsp.
Baking Soda	2 tsp.
Buttermilk	1/2 cup
Applesauce	1/2 cup
Walnuts	1/2 cup, chopped
Blackberries	1 1/2 cup, wild

Cream butter and sugar together, beat in eggs one at a time until fluffy. Sift dry ingredients together and mix into creamed mixture. Dissolve baking soda in buttermilk. Alternately, stir the buttermilk mixture and the applesauce into the batter. Fold in blackberries and nuts. Bake in a 9" x 13" pan at 350° for 55 minutes. Serve plain or with whipped cream.

Serves: 12 - 14

Mary Lou Muth
Auburn, Wa

COBBLERS

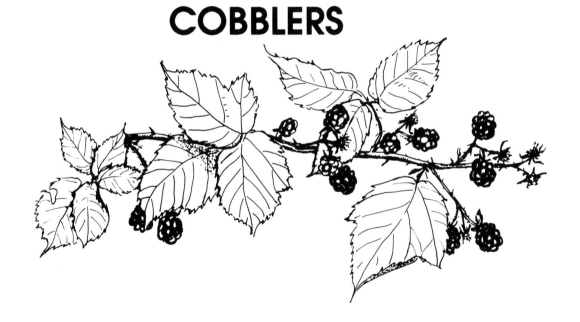

Baked Blackberry Dessert

Blackberries	2 cups
Sugar	1 1/4 cups, divided
Flour	1 3/4 cups, sifted
Baking Powder	2 1/2 tsp.
Salt	1/2 tsp.
Butter	1/2 cup
Egg	1
Vanilla	1 tsp.
Milk	1/2 cup
Sweet Cream	For topping

Pre-heat oven to 350°.

Sift together flour, baking powder and salt. Cream together butter, 3/4 cup sugar, and beat in egg and vanilla. Add flour mixture alternately with the milk to the butter mixture and mix thoroughly. Place berries and remaining 1/2 cup sugar in buttered baking dish. Pour batter over berries and bake 50 minutes. Serve with sweet cream if desired.

Serves 6

Jean Baker
Bothell, WA

Blackberry Cobbler

Blackberries	4 - 5 cups
Water	3/4 - 1 cup (depends on desired juiciness of cobbler)
Sugar	1 1/4 cups, divided
Cornstarch	1 1/2 - 2 Tbsp.
Flour	1 cup
Baking Powder	1 tsp.
Egg	1, beaten
Melted Butter or Margarine	3 - 4 Tbsp.
Cinnamon	1/2 tsp.

Combine clean berries with water in a saucepan. Bring to a boil. Combine 1/2 cup sugar with the cornstarch and add to the berries. Cook and stir mixture until thickened. Pour berry mixture into a 8" x 8" pan or a 2 quart glass casserole. Mix flour, remaining sugar, baking powder and salt in a bowl. Add beaten egg and mix with a fork until crumbly. Spread over berries and drizzle with melted butter. Sprinkle with cinnamon and bake at 350° for approximately 30 min.

Shirley Patterson
Carnation, WA

Brennan's Blackberry Custard Cobbler

Sugar	1 cup
Blackberries	4 cups
Flour	1 Tbsp.
Eggs	3

Mix eggs, sugar and flour and carefully fold in berries. Put in a buttered baking dish. Make Topping.

Butter	1 cube (1/2 cup)
Sugar	1/2 cup
Flour	1 1/2 cup

Melt butter, add sugar and blend in flour. Drop topping by the spoonful on top of berry mixture and bake approximately 35 minutes at 375°. Serve plain or with whipped cream.

Serves 6 - 8

Beth Brennan-Claseman
Seattle, WA

Corn Berry Cobbler

Blackberries	1 quart
Honey	3/4 cup, divided
Cornmeal	1 cup
Baking Powder	1 tsp.
Salt	1/2 tsp.
Melted Butter	4 Tbsp., divided
Buttermilk or Yogurt	1/2 cup
Lemon Juice	1 Tbsp.

Pre-heat oven to 350°.

Arrange berries in a buttered 2 quart baking dish and drizzle them with 1/4 cup of honey. Mix together cornmeal, baking powder, salt, buttermilk or yogurt and 2 Tbs. of melted butter. Drop batter, by tablespoonful, onto berries. Mix together the remaining honey, butter, and lemon juice and pour over top of the batter. Bake for approximately one hour. Serve warm.

Serves: 6 - 8

Vivian Schnorr
Stanwood, WA

Blackberry Marble Cobbler

Sugar	1 cup, divided
Flour	1 cup
Baking Powder	2 tsp.
Salt	1/4 tsp.
Milk	1/2 cup
Vanilla	1/2 tsp.
Melted Butter	1 Tbsp.
Blackberries	1 cup
Boiling Water	3/4 cup
Ice Cream or Whipped Cream for topping	

Sift together into bowl: 1/2 cup sugar, flour, baking powder and salt. Stir in milk, vanilla and melted butter. Spread batter in a buttered 10" x 6" baking dish. Scatter berries over batter and sprinkle 1/2 cup sugar over the berries. Pour the boiling water over all and bake at 375° for 25 - 30 minutes until well browned and done. Top with ice cream or whipped cream if desired.

Serves 6

Marian Tague
Indianola, WA

Wild Blackberry Cobbler

Blackberries	3 cups
Sugar	1 1/2 cups, divided
Lemon Juice	1/2 tsp.
Butter	Approx. 1 Tbsp.
Salt	1/2 tsp.
Baking Powder	2 tsp.
Flour	1 cup
Egg	1, beaten
Milk	1/2 cup
Melted Butter	3 Tbsp.

Mix berries with 1 cup of sugar and lemon juice, pour into well greased baking dish. Dot with butter. Sift together salt, baking powder, and flour and set aside. Combine beaten egg, remaining sugar, milk and melted butter, add to dry ingredients, mixing thoroughly. Cover berries with batter and bake at 375° for approximately 30 minutes. Serve warm, plain or with whipped cream.

Serves 6 - 8

Mary Lou Muth
Auburn, WA

CREPES

Basic Recipe for Rolled or Folded Crepes

Eggs	2
Milk	1 cup
Salt	pinch
Flour	1 cup
Cognac	2 tsp.
Butter	2 tsp., melted

Mix ingredients thoroughly with whisk and let stand for 1 to 2 hours. (The batter should be of the consistency to just coat the spoon. If batter is too thick, add more milk.) Heat pan, add a little clarified butter and pour in 1 - 2 Tbs. of batter. Tilt the pan so batter spreads over the entire pan bottom. Cook quickly on both sides. Repeat the process until all batter is used, stacking crepes on a plate as they are cooked. This recipe makes 18 - 20 crepes. Place a spoonful or two of filling across each crepe and roll up. A serving is 2 or 3 crepes with filling. The filled crepes can be topped with sprinkled powder sugar, ice cream or lemon curd.

Erika Norwood
Seattle, WA

Blackberry Fillings for Crepes

Fresh Blackberry Filling

Blackberries	3 cups
Sugar	1/2 cup (or to taste)
Water	2 Tbsp.
Cornstarch	1 1/2 - 2 tsp.
Cinnamon	dash (optional)

Mash half the blackberries in a saucepan and add sugar. Dissolve cornstarch in the water.   Add the water-cornstarch mixture to the blackberries and sugar. Cook, stirring constantly, until mixture thickens. Remove from heat, cool, and gently stir in the remaining blackberries.

Makes about 2 cups.

Blackberry Cream Filling

Sugar	4 Tbsp.
Flour	2 Tbsp.
Eggs	2
Whole Milk	1 cup, hot
Blackberries	1 1/2 cup
Vanilla or Cognac	1/2 tsp.

Combine all ingredients except blackberries and flavoring in the top half of a double boiler and cook over hot water, stirring constantly, until the mixture is thick and smooth. Remove from heat and stir in the vanilla or cognac. Cool mixture before adding berries.

Fill rolled or folded crepes.

Blackberry Apple Filling (for Crepes)

Butter or Margarine	4 Tbsp.
Tart Apples	1 1/2 cups (peeled and chopped)
Blackberries	2 cups
Sugar	1/2 cup
White Wine or Apple Cider	1/2 cup
Cornstarch	1 1/2 tsp.

Gently cook chopped apples in butter until tender. Add blackberries and sugar, stirring to dissolve sugar. Dissolve the cornstarch in the wine or cider and add to the berry mixture. Bring to a boil, lower heat and cook for a few minutes to thicken. Cool and use as a filling for crepes.

Makes enough to fill twelve 6 inch crepes.

Gwen's Blackberry Crepes

Crepes:

Eggs	3, beaten
Milk	2 cups
Vegetable Oil	2 Tbsp.
Flour	2 cups

Mix all ingredients together until batter is consistency of heavy cream. Rest batter for 1/2 to 1 hour.

Sauce:

Wild Blackberry Jam	1 cup
Fresh or frozen Wild Blackberries	1 cup

In a small sauce pan, over medium heat, combine jam and berries. If sauce seems too thick, thin with water. Keep warm.

Butter	
Whipping Cream or Creme Fraiche	As garnish

In a 6 to 8 inch crepe pan melt 1 tsp. butter. Add 2 to 3 Tbsp. batter and tilt to cover bottom of pan with a thin layer of batter. Cook until edges are browned. Turn and cook other side for a few seconds. Remove to a warm plate. Repeat for more crepes.

Spoon about 2 Tbsp. of filling in center of crepe and roll. Place seam side down. Top with additional sauce and garnish with cream if desired. You may also sift powdered sugar over the top of the crepes.

Makes 16 crepes

Gwen Van Horn
San Juan Island, WA.

FROZEN DESSERTS

Blackberry Ice

Water	2 cups
Sugar	1 cup
Blackberry Juice	2 cups
Lemon Juice	1/4 cup

Boil water with sugar for 5 minutes. Add blackberry juice and lemon juice. Cool and freeze the mixture in either refrigerator trays or an ice cream freezer.

Ices, like ice cream, may be frozen in trays or an ice cream maker. Also like ice cream, ices need to be beaten or whipped with a whisk during the freezing process, for smoothness. If the ice is made in trays, beat it thoroughly every half hour while freezing. Allow the finished ice to stand in the freezer to mellow for a few hours.

Blackberry Ice Cream

Sugar	2 Tbsp.
Salt	Pinch
Cinnamon	1/8 tp.
Cornstarch	1/4 cup
Milk	1 1/2 cups
Blackberries	1 1/2 - 2 cups
Heavy Cream	1 1/4 cup

In saucepan combine sugar, salt, cinnamon and cornstarch. Gradually blend in milk. Cook over low heat, stirring constantly, until thickened. Cool slightly. Force blackberries through a sieve and sweeten the resulting puree to taste. Pour the cooled cooked mixture into a blender, add the blackberry puree and heavy cream. Blend at low speed for 60 seconds and chill in refrigerator 2 to 3 hours. Freeze mixture in an ice cream maker according to manufacturers directions. Mixture can also be frozen in refrigerator trays but must be stirred several times during the freezing process.

Geannie Kuranko's Blackberry Ice Cream

Milk	1 Quart
Sugar	2 1/4 cups divided
Flour	1/4 cup
Salt	1/2 tsp.
Eggs	4, beaten
Almond or Blackberry Flavoring	1 Tbsp.
Light Cream	1 1/2 quarts
(1 can of milk + whole milk to equal 1 1/2 quarts can also be used.)	
Blackberries	1 pint
Rock Salt	
Crushed Ice	

Mix 2 cups sugar, flour and salt together. Scald milk and add enough hot milk to sugar-flour mixture to make a thin paste. Stir paste into remaining hot milk and cook over low heat until mixture thickens (about 15 minutes). Cool mixture in refrigerator.

Mix blackberries with 1/4 cup sugar and let stand for about 20 minutes to form a syrup. When cooked mixture has cooled, pour into a 1 1/2 gallon ice cream freezer, add flavoring, light cream and blackberry syrup. Pack freezer with ice and rock salt and churn until frozen.

Geannie Kuranko
South Prairie, WA

Frozen Blackberry Pudding

Crust:

Chopped Nuts	3/4 cup
Flour	1 1/4 cups
Brown Sugar	1/4 cup
Melted Butter	1/2 cup

Filling:

Blackberries	2 cups
Egg Whites	2
Lemon Juice	2 Tbsp.
Sugar	1 cup
Cool Whip	1 8 oz. pkg.

Mix nuts, flour, brown sugar and melted butter together and spread evenly in a 9 x 13" baking pan. Bake at 350° for 20 min., stirring after 10 min. Reserve 1/4 cup of this toasted crust for a garnish to sprinkle on top. Press remaining mixture back in pan to cool.

Beat egg whites until stiff. Add sugar and beat again. Add lemon juice and beat until mixed. Fold in blackberries gently and then Cool Whip. Spread berry mixture on crust. Sprinkle with remaining crumbs and freeze.

JAMS & JELLIES

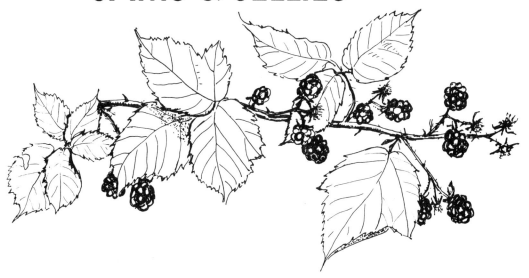

Blackberry Jam

Blackberries	3 pounds
Sugar	2 1/2 pounds
	(4 1/2 cups)

Alternate layers of blackberries and sugar in a large pot or preserving kettle. Let stand at least one hour before cooking. Cook slowly until thick. Pour into sterilized glasses and seal. Makes 3 pints.

Jean Baker
Bothell, WA

Brazil Nut-Blackberry Conserve

Blackberry Juice	4 cups
Sugar	7 1/2 cups
Water	1/4 cup
Brazil Nuts	1 cup, chopped
Fruit Pectin	1 cup

Combine juice and water. Cook and stir until mixture boils. Cover and simmer 15 minutes. Add sugar and mix well. Heat mixture rapidly to the boiling point. Add fruit pectin and nuts. Boil mixture for 1 minute before pouring into sterilized glasses.

Jean Baker
Bothell, WA

Blackberry Jam Without Pectin*

Blackberries	**2 1/2 pounds**
Sugar	**1 1/2 pounds**

Wash berries and drain thoroughly. In a large pot, crush
the berries and heat them until they boil, stirring constantly.
Add sugar and cook rapidly until mixture tests for jelly. To
test for jelly, remove a little cooked juice, cool it slightly
and slowly pour it back into the pot from the edge of the
spoon. When the drops run together and fall from the
spoon in a sheet, leaving the edge of the spoon clean,
the jam is ready. Pour into sterile jars and seal.

* Many berries do not need the addition of commercial
pectin to jell. You can rely on the fruit's natural pectin.
(There is more natural pectin in underripe berries.) For
another natural source of pectin, you can add the peels of
3 or 4 tart apples. If your jam fails to jell, use it as a sauce
over ice cream, waffles, pancakes or crepes.

Freezer Blackberry Jam

Powdered Pectin	1 pkg.
Sugar	4 1/2 cups
Light Corn Syrup	1 cup
Lemon Juice	1/4 cup
Blackberries	3 1/4 cups

Wash and crush berries. Put the measured crushed fruit and lemon juice into a 4 quart kettle. Sift in 1 pkg. powdered pectin. Stir vigorously and let stand for 30 minutes.

Add corn syrup and mix well. Measure the sugar into a dry bowl and add gradually to the crushed fruit. Warming slightly - not above 100° F, will hasten sugar dissolving. Jam is ready when sugar is dissolved.

Pour into jelly glasses or freezer containers and cover. Jam will keep in refrigerator for 2 or 3 weeks. Store in freezer for longer periods.

Makes 7 cups.

Blackberry Jelly Without Added Pectin

Blackberry Juice	**4 cups**
(About 2 1/2 Qts. berries and 3/4 cup water)	
Sugar	**3 cups**

To prepare juice, select one fourth underripe and three fourths ripe berries. Sort and wash; remove stems. Crush berries, add water, cover and bring to a boil on high heat. Reduce heat and simmer for 5 minutes. Put into a damp jelly bag or into a colander lined with muslin, and extract juice. The clearest jelly comes from juice that has dripped through the bag without pressing. Greater yield of juice, however, can be obtained by twisting the bag of fruit tightly and squeezing or pressing juice through.

Measure juice into kettle; add sugar and stir well. Boil over high heat until jelly mixture sheets from spoon.

Remove from heat; skim off foam. Pour jelly into hot jars and seal.

Makes about 5 six-ounce glasses.

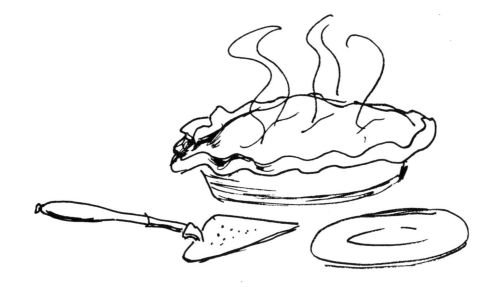

PIES & PASTRIES

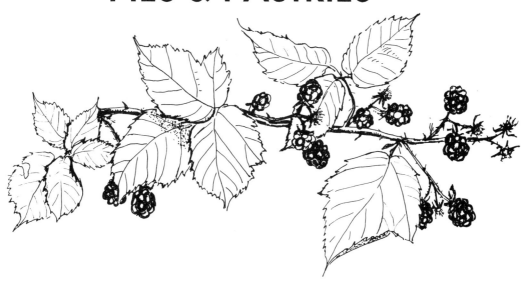

Blackberry Pie

Baked Pie Shell	1 - 9"
Blackberries	4 cups
Sugar	1 cup
Water	1 cup
Cornstarch	2 1/2 Tbsp.
Blackberry Jello	3 Tbsp. (dry)

Mix together sugar, water and cornstarch. Cook mixture until clear. Stir in Jello powder and stir until dissolved. Let mixture cool slightly, then mix with blackberries. Pour into baked shell. Chill pie in refrigerator until ready to serve. Serve with whipped cream.

70

Leona Robertson   &   Carolyn Savitteri
Sedro Wooley, WA   Tempe, AZ

Wild and Free Blackberry Pie

Blackberries	3 cups
Sugar	1 cup
Flour	2 Tbsp.
Lemon Juice	2 Tbsp.
Ground Cinnamon	1/4 tsp.
Butter or Margarine	1 Tbsp.
Pastry	For 2 crust 9" pie

Pre-heat oven to 450°

Combine blackberries, sugar, flour, lemon juice and cinnamon. Line pie pan with 1/2 of pie crust. Add fruit mixture to pie pan and dot with butter. Cover with top crust and cut slits in top crust to allow steam to escape while baking. Bake at 450° for 10 minutes; reduce temperature to 350° and bake 25-30 minutes longer, or until crust begins to brown.

Blackberry-Apple Pie

Blackberries	**2 cups**
Apples	**2 cups**
(peeled, cored and chopped)	
Sugar	**1 cup**
Salt	**dash**
Flour	**4 Tbsp.**
Pastry	**for 2 crust 8" pie**

Prepare crust. Line 8" pie pan with 1/2 of crust, prick bottom with fork. Place blackberries and apples into pie pan. Cover with a mixture of sugar, salt and flour. Cover with top crust, crimp edges and make slits in top to allow steam to escape during baking. Bake at 400° for 10 minutes. Reduce heat to 375° and bake an additional 20 - 30 minutes until brown and bubbly. Cool before serving.

Mary McLaren
Auburn, WA

Blackberry Cheesecake Pie

Pie Crust	1

Filling:

Sour Cream	1/2 cup
Cream Cheese	8 oz. softened
Sugar	1/3 cup
Eggs	2
Vanilla	1 tsp.

Combine softened cream cheese and sour cream in a bowl. Mix at medium speed until smooth. Add sugar, eggs and vanilla. Mix well and pour into pie crust. Bake at 375° for 25 - 30 minutes. Cool thoroughly before covering with topping.

Topping:

Sugar	1/2 - 3/4 cup
Cornstarch	3 Tbsp.
Cranberry Juice Cocktail	3/4 - 1 cup
Blackberries	3 - 4 cups

Combine sugar and cornstarch in saucepan; stir in cranberry cocktail and stir to dissolve cornstarch. Cook over medium heat until thick and transparent. Cool slightly and stir in berries. Spoon on cooled pie and refrigerate 2 or 3 hours until topping is set.

Wild Blackberry Delight Pie

Double Pie Crust	1
Wild Blackberries	3 1/2 cups
Raspberries	3/4 cup
Boysenberries	3/4 cup
Sugar	1 cup
Minute Tapioca	2 Tbsp.

Pre-heat oven to 400°

Place all berries in bowl, add sugar and tapioca. Let stand. Drain excess juice from bowl of berries. Place drained fruit onto bottom crust. Put on top crust

Bake for 20 minutes. Reduce heat to 350° and continue baking for 30 - 35 minutes or until lightly browned. Serve with your favorite vanilla ice cream.

Barbara Doolin
Woodinville WA

Blackberry Dream Pie

Baked Pie Shell	1, 10 inch
Blackberries	2 cups
Unflavored Gelatin	2 packages
Orange Juice Concentrate	1/2 cup
Cinnamon	1/4 tsp.
Honey	1 tsp.
Orange Peel	2 tsp. (grated)
Fresh Whole Berries	1 quart

Cook 2 cups blackberries until hot and very juicy. Put berries through a food mill or strain through cheesecloth. Dissolve gelatin in hot blackberry juice, add orange juice concentrate, orange peel, cinnamon and honey. Stir well and cool mixture. Pile one quart blackberries in the baked, cooled pie shell and pour the cooled, slightly thickened juice mixture over the berries. Refrigerate for several hours before serving. Garnish with whipped cream if desired.

Blackberry Cream Pie

Blackberries	4 cups
Sugar	1 1/2 cups
Baking Soda	1/2 tsp.
Butter	2 Tbsp.
Cornstarch	3 Tbsp.
Water	1/4 cup
Pie Shell	1 - 8", baked
Whipping Cream	1 cup, whipped

Combine blackberries, sugar, baking soda and butter in a medium saucepan and cook over medium heat until mixture boils. Combine cornstarch with water, add to berry mixture and continue cooking until mixture becomes very thick. Cool slightly; pour into pie shell and chill. Before serving, cover pie with whipped cream.

Mary McLaren
Auburn, WA

Eleanor's Favorite Blackberry Pie

Baked Pie Crust	1
Blackberries	1 - 1 1/2 cups
Sugar	To taste
Cornstarch	1 - 2 tsp.
Water	2 Tbsp.
Blackberries	2 - 3 cups
Whipped Cream	As garnish

Dissolve the cornstarch in water. Cook 1 - 1 1/2 cups blackberries with the dissolved cornstarch and sugar over low heat, stirring constantly, until mixture thickens. Cool slightly.

Pile 2 - 3 cups blackberries into baked pie crust. Spoon cooked and cooled mixture over fresh berries and refrigerate for several hours. Garnish as desired with whipped cream.

Louise Cooper's Blackberry Pie

Blackberries	**4 cups**
Sugar	**1 cup**
Flour	**1/2 cup**
Cinnamon	**1/2 tsp.**
Butter	**1 1/2 Tbsp.**
Pastry	**for two crust 9" pie**

Mix blackberries lightly with sugar, flour and cinnamon. Pour into pastry lined pie pan, dot with butter. Cover with top crust and crimp. Bake at 400° for first 15 minutes, then turn oven down to 350° and bake 40 minutes more.

A. Louise Cooper
Woodinville, WA

Sour Cream Blackberry Pie

Brown Sugar	1/2 cup
Tapioca	3 Tbsp.
Egg,	1, beaten
Egg white	1
Salt	pinch
Sour Cream	1 cup
Blackberries	3 cups
9 inch Pie Shell	1

Pre-heat oven to 450°.

Combine egg, sour cream, sugar, salt and tapioca in a bowl. Brush pie shell lightly with beaten egg white. Fill shell with the berries and cover with egg-sour cream mixture. Bake the pie at 450° for 10 minutes. Reduce temperature to 325° and continue baking for 30 to 35 minutes.

Blackberry Preserve Cream Cheese Pastry

Cream Cheese	1 - 3 ounce package
Blackberry Jam or Preserves	1/2 cup
Butter	1/4 cup
Biscuit Mix	2 cups
Milk	1/3 cup

In a mixing bowl cut cream cheese and butter into biscuit mix until crumbly. Blend in milk with a spoon. Place on floured surface and knead 10-12 times. Roll dough on waxed paper into a 12x18 inch rectangle. Remove waxed paper and place on a greased baking sheet. Spread jam down the center of the dough, 3" x 10". Make 2 1/2" cuts at 1" intervals on long sides of the rectangle of dough. Overlap and fold strips over jam and bake at 425° for 12-15 minutes. Drizzle confectioners icing over warm pastry.

Carrie Duwe
Bainbridge Island, WA

Blackberry Fritters

Flour	3/4 cup, sifted
Sugar	2 Tbsp.
Water or Milk	1/4 cup
Butter	1 Tbsp., melted
Brandy or White Wine	2 Tbsp.
Salt	Pinch
Egg	1, separated
Blackberries	2 cups
Oil for deep frying	

Combine flour, sugar, milk or water and melted butter. Stir in brandy or wine, salt, and a well-beaten egg yolk. (The batter should be the consistancy of thick cream.) Fold in stiffly beaten egg white and gently add dry blackberries. Drop batter by the spoonful into hot oil. Cook until fritters are golden brown on both sides, about 3 - 5 minutes. Drain fritters on absorbent paper. Serve with powdered sugar.

Wild Blackberry Pinwheels

Flour	2 cups
Salt	1/2 tsp.
Baking Powder	4 tsp.
Sugar	3 Tbsp. divided
Shortening	1/3 cup
Egg	1, well beaten
Milk	2/3 cup
Butter	1 Tbsp., melted
Cinnamon	dash
Blackberries	2 cups, mashed, juice extracted and saved

Sift together flour, salt, baking powder and 1 Tbsp. sugar. Cut in shortening until mixture forms coarse crumbs. Add egg and milk. Blend well and turn out on floured surface. Knead dough lightly and roll to 1/2" thick. Brush with melted butter. Sprinkle dough with 2 Tbsp. sugar and dash of cinnamon. Spread dough with mashed blackberries and roll dough up. Cut into 9 slices and place on top of blackberry mixture.

Blackberry Mixture

Flour	2 Tbsp.
Sugar	1/4 cup
Blackberries	2 cups

Blend flour, sugar, blackberries and juice saved from pinwheels in a saucepan and cook until thick. Pour mixture into 8'"square baking pan. Cover with Blackberry Pinwheels and bake 20 minutes at 425° Serve hot with cream.

Bettie Fowler
Seattle, WA.

Blackberry Roly Poly*

Flour	2 cups
Baking Powder	2 tsp.
Salt	1/2 tsp.
Sugar	1 cup + 1 Tbsp.
Nutmeg or Cinnamon	pinch
Butter	4 Tbsp.
Milk	3/4 cup
Butter	2 Tbsp., melted
Blackberries	6 cups

Pre-heat oven to 425º.

Sift together flour, baking powder, salt, 1 Tbs. sugar and nutmeg or cinnamon. Cut in butter until crumbly and add milk, little by little, until the dough holds together. Roll or pat out dough into an oblong shape about 1/2 inch thick. Mix the blackberries with 1 cup sugar and put 1/2 of the blackberries over the rolled out dough. Roll dough up like a jelly roll and put the roll, seam side down, into a 8 x 12" pan. Put the rest of the sugared berries around the roll and bake for 30 minutes. Cut into slices and serve with cream or sauce.

Erika Norwood
Seattle, WA

*Roly Poly - Any dessert made from a stiff dough spread thin, then topped with fruit, rolled jelly roll fashion and baked, steamed or simmered. Roly Poly's originated in England and was traditionally made with a suet dough, spread with sweet syrup or jam and boiled.

PUDDINGS

Baked Blackberry Pudding

Blackberries	**4 cups**
Butter	**1/4 cup**
Sugar	**1/2 cup**
Egg	**1**
Sifted Flour	**1 1/2 cups, divided**
Baking Powder	**2 tsp.**
Salt	**1/4 tsp.**

Wash blackberries and spread 2 cups of the berries in a single layer to dry. Heat remaining 2 cups of berries for a few minutes and press out juice. There should be 1/2 cup juice. If not, add water to make 1/2 cup. Cream butter and sugar together, add egg and mix well. Sift the dry ingredients together reserving 2 Tbs. flour to coat the dry berries. Add the dry ingredients, alternating with the pressed berries, to the creamed butter mixture. Fold in the floured berries and bake in a well greased tube pan for approximately 1 hour at 300-325°, bake longer if needed. Serve hot or cold, plain or with whipped cream.

Serves: 8

Mrs. Agatha C. Volk
Tacoma, WA

Blackberry Clafouti *

Blackberries	**3 cups**
Milk	**1 1/4 cups**
Sugar	**2/3 cups, divided**
Eggs	**3**
Vanilla Extract	**1 Tbsp.**
Salt	**pinch**
Sifted Flour	**1 1/4 cups**
Powdered Sugar	**to taste**

Pre-heat oven to 350°.

Put milk, 1/3 cup sugar, eggs, vanilla, salt and flour into blender jar. Cover and blend on high speed for 1 minute. Pour a 1/4 inch layer of this batter into a buttered 7 or 8 cup oven-proof baking dish or deep pie plate. Set pan over a moderate heat for a minute until batter has set in the bottom of the dish. Remove from heat and spread berries on batter. Sprinkle with the remaining 1/3 cup sugar and then pour remaining batter over all. Spread evenly and bake for about an hour until Clafouti is puffed and brown. Sprinkle top with powdered sugar. Should be served hot or warm and it will sink slightly when cooled.

Serves 6 - 8

*Clafouti:
A simple seasonal French dessert originating in the Limousin region - essentially fruit baked in a thin pancake like batter, traditionally made with sweet cherries.

Blackberry and Cream Mousse

Unflavored Gelatin	1 Tbsp.
Cold Water	2 Tbsp.
Blackberry Juice	1/4 cup.
Cream Cheese	8 ounces, softened
Sugar	1/2 cup
Blackberries	1 cup, pureed
	1 cup, whole
Whipped Cream	1 1/4 cup
Vanilla	1/2 tsp.
Grand Marnier	1 Tbsp.

Sprinkle gelatin over 2 Tbsp. water to soften. Heat blackberry juice and stir in softened gelatin, stirring to dissolve. Whip cream cheese until fluffy. Add sugar, pureed berries and juice-gelatin mixture to cream cheese. Beat well on medium speed. Fold in whole berries.

In separate bowl whip cream until stiff and add vanilla and Grand Mariner. Fold this mixture into blackberry mixture and spoon into serving glasses.

Serves 6 - 8

Adrianne J. Flint
Lynnwood, Washington

Blackberry Custard

Blackberries	4 cups
Butter	1 cup
Sugar	1 1/2 cups
Stale Sponge Cake	1 loaf, crumbled
Egg Yolks	6, beaten
Egg Whites	6, beaten very stiff

Simmer blackberries for a few minutes. Cool. Cream butter and sugar and add berries. Add the sponge cake and the egg yolks. Fold in egg whites. Bake in buttered baking dish for 35 minutes at 375°. Serve warm with ice cream or whipped cream.

Mary Lou Muth
Auburn, WA

Blackberry Dumplings

Blackberries	3 quarts
Sugar	1 1/2 - 2 cups
Water	
Biscuit Mix	2 cups
Milk	2/3 cup
Sugar	(depends on sweetness of berries and taste preference.)

Fill a 6 quart pot half full of blackberries. Add sugar (to taste) and add water even with the top of the berries. Bring to a boil.

To make dumplings, combine biscuit mix, milk and sugar. Drop dumplings by the spoonful into blackberry mixture and cook for 20 minutes over low heat. Serve warm, plain or with cream.

Mrs. Florence Monroe
Redmond, WA

Blackberry Compote

Sugar	1/2 cup
Cinnamon Stick	one small
Rind of 1 Lemon	grated
Blackberries	1 quart
Orange-flavored Liqueur	2 Tbsp.

Put berries, sugar, cinnamon stick and grated lemon rind in a large saucepan. Bring to a boil and simmer gently for 2 or 3 minutes. Remove from heat. Remove cinnamon stick and add orange-flavored liqueur. Chill and serve over ice cream or in dessert dishes topped with whipped cream.

Makes about 4 cups.

Blackberry Flummery*

Blackberries	2 cups
Water	2 cups
Sugar	1 cup
Cornstarch	1/4 cup
Salt	1/4 tsp.
Lemon Juice	1 Tbsp.

Simmer blackberries and water in a saucepan for 15 minutes until berries soften. Combine sugar, cornstarch and salt in a bowl and blend well. Gradually stir sugar mixture into berries, bring to a boil, while stirring, and let mixture simmer for 5 minutes, stirring often. Remove from heat and add lemon juice, stir again. Serve warm with cream.

Jean Baker
Bothell, WA

* **Flummery:** Traditionally an old English and Irish sweet pudding made of oatmeal with fruit, nuts, cream and a flavoring. Currently used to mean a simple berry concoction - boiled, sweetened and thickened.

Blackberry Fool *

Blackberries	2 cups
Sugar	1/2 cup, or to taste
Lemon Juice	2 drops
Heavy Cream	1 cup, whipped

Puree the blackberries, stir the sugar and lemon juice into the puree. Pour into a glass serving bowl. Using a spatula, lightly fold the whipped cream into the puree, combining the ingredients so there is a contrast of flavor and color. Chill well.

Serves: 4

***Fool:** A dessert made with pureed fruit, raw or cooked, sweetened and mixed with either whipped egg whites or whipped cream - served with sweet biscuits or cookies.

Blackberry Grunt*

Blackberries	4 cups, washed
Sugar	1 cup + 2 Tbsp., divided
Water	1/2 cup
Butter	1 1/2 Tbsp.
Flour	1 cup
Baking Powder	1 1/2 tsp.
Salt	dash
Milk	1/2 cup
Melted Butter	2 Tbsp.

Combine the berries, 1 cup sugar, water and butter in a heat-proof casserole dish that can be used on the top of the stove. Bring to a boil. In a separate bowl, mix the flour, baking powder, salt, remaining sugar, milk and melted butter. Spoon this mixture over the berry mixture and cover the dish tightly. Simmer for 12 minutes. When mixture is cooked, a knife inserted in the topping, will come out clean. Serve warm, with cream.

*Grunt: A dessert made by dropping dough on boiling berries, covering and steaming.

Blackberry Pudding Flint

Blackberries	2 cups
Sugar	1/2 - 1 cup
Water	2 cups
Biscuits	4 - 5, crumbled
Butter	1 Tbsp.

Bring blackberries, sugar and water to a near boil in a buttered baking dish. Add the crumbled biscuits and stir. Dot with butter, sprinkle with sugar (if desired) and bake at 400° until thick and glossy on top.

Adrianne J. Flint
Lynnwood, WA

Blackberry Pudding With Sauce

Butter	1/2 cup
Sugar	1 cup
Eggs	2, beaten
Milk	1/2 cup
Blackberries	1/2 cup or more
Baking Soda	1/2 tsp.
Flour	1/2 cup
Baking Powder	1 tsp.

Cream together butter and sugar, add beaten eggs. Sift together dry ingredients and add to creamed mixture alternately with the milk. Fold in blackberries. Bake at 375° for 30-35 minutes, or until toothpick comes out clean. Serve with sauce.

Sauce

Blackberries	1 cup
Sugar	to taste
Cornstarch	1 tsp.

Crush blackberries to extract juice. Sweeten berry and juice mixture to taste, with sugar. Cook for a few minutes with cornstarch until sauce is thickened.

Serves 6

Mrs. H. B. Wallace
Carnation, WA

Blackberry Trifle

Blackberries	3 cups
Sugar	1/2 cup
Cornstarch	2 tsp.
Ladyfingers	1 package
Madeira or sweet Sherry	2 Tbsp.
Vanilla Pudding	made according to directions (or make your own).
Blackberry Jam	As needed

Mix sugar with cornstarch in a sauce pan. Add blackberries and cook, stirring constantly for a few minutes until mixture is syrupy and slightly thickened. Cool slightly.

Split ladyfingers and spread them with jam. Place half of the ladyfingers on the bottom of an attractive bowl or dish and sprinkle with the wine. Cover the ladyfingers with half of the blackberries and then with half of the pudding. Put another layer of ladyfingers on the pudding, then the rest of the berries and pudding. Refrigerate, preferable overnight. Decorate before serving, with whipped cream.

Serves 6 - 8.

SAUCES, SOUPS & SYRUPS

Geannie Kuranko's Blackberry Syrup

Blackberry Juice	**1 1/4 cups**
Sugar	**1 1/4 cups**
Light Corn Syrup	**1/2 cup**

Extract juice from blackberries and combine with sugar and corn syrup in a large pan. Bring mixture to a full rolling boil. Boil for 1 minute. Remove mixture from heat, skim off foam and pour into clean, hot jars. Cover jars with lids and tighten. Process jars for 10 minutes in boiling water bath.

Makes 2 cups

Geannie Kuranko
South Prairie, WA

Blackberry Syrup

Blackberries	**approximately 1 cup**
Sugar	**to taste**

Heat blackberries slightly, add sugar and stir until mixture is syrupy. Spoon over ice cream while syrup is still warm.

Makes 1 cup

A. Louise Cooper
Woodinville, WA.

Cold Blackberry Soup

Blackberries	**2 cups**
Sugar	**1/3 cup**
Sour Cream	**1/2 cup**
Heavy Sweet Cream	**1/2 cup**
Water	**1 1/2 cups**
Light Red or Rose' wine	**1/2 cup**

Place berries in a blender and puree. Strain if desired. Add sugar and stir until dissolved. Stir in both creams, water and wine. Stir well and pour into pitcher and chill well before serving.

Makes 4 servings of about 1 cup each

Blackberry Soup

Blackberries	**4 cups**
Water	**1 1/2 - 2 cups**
Lemon	**1/2**
Sugar	**1/4 cup**
Cloves	**2 or 3**
Cinnamon	**2 In. stick**
Cream or Half and Half	**1/2 cup**

Simmer berries with water, lemon, sugar and spices in a kettle until fruit is very soft. Strain through a sieve to separate juice and pulp from seeds. Cool, chill and add cream or Half and Half.

Serves 6-8

A Very Versatile Blackberry Sauce

Blackberries	3 cups
Sugar	1/2 cup
	or to taste
Lime	1, juice and rind
Cornstarch	4 tsp. dissolved
	in 1/4 cup water
Orange Flavored Liqueur	2 Tbsp.

Cook berries with sugar until very liquid. Add cornstarch dissolved in water and cook, stirring constantly, over medium heat until thickened. Add juice and grated rind of lime, and liqueur.

This sauce may be varied according to taste and use. You may substitute lemon, orange or apple juice for the lime. For filling crepes or cream puffs, or for individual pre-baked pie shells, thicken it further with another tsp. of cornstarch .

Make it thinner with less cornstarch or a bit more water for saucing ice cream, puddings, pound cake, cheesecakes, dessert omelets, popovers or soufflés.

Blackberry Vinegar

Blackberries	**4 cups**
Rice Vinegar	**1 1/2 cups**
Sugar	**1/4 cup per cup of liquid**

Place blackberries in narrow crock or a wide mouth one quart jar. Crush berries slightly and pour vinegar over berries to cover. Add more vinegar to cover berries completely, if necessary. Let stand in a cool place for 24 - 36 hours, or for five days if placed in a refrigerator. Stir mixture at least once a day.

Strain mixture through a double thickness of cheesecloth, collecting juice in a bowl. Press berries lightly to get all possible juice. Juice should equal 3 1/2 cups of liquid. Pour liquid into a saucepan and add 1/4 cup sugar for each cup of liquid. Heat mixture to a gentle boil over medium heat, then reduce heat and simmer, uncovered, for five minutes, skimming the surface when necessary.

If the vinegar is to be used within a few weeks, pour vinegar into clean dry jars, cap tightly, and store in the refrigerator. If the vinegar is to be stored for a longer period of time, pour into hot, sterilized jars, cap tightly and store at room temperature.

* Wine or cider vinegar can be substituted for the rice vinegar.

Stewed Blackberries (Diet)

Blackberries	2 cups
Water	1/2 cup
Liquid Sweetener	1 Tbsp.
Lemon Juice	1/2 tsp.

Wash berries in cold water. Place berries in pan, add water, cover and simmer for 15 minutes. Add lemon juice and sweetener and simmer 3 minutes. Stir several times during cooking. Cool and serve.

Serves 5.

Gwen Van Horn
San Juan Island, WA

NOTES

NOTES

INDEX

Bibliography

Angier, Bradford, 1972. _Feasting Free on Wild Edibles._ Stackpole Books, Harrisburg, PA.

Bainbridge Review. October 2 and 16, 1985.

Cuisine Magazine. July, 1982.

Fulweiler, Kyle D., 1985. _The Berry Cookbook._ Pacific Search Press, Seattle.

Hitchcock, C. Leo, and Cronquist, Arthur. 1973. _Flora of the Pacific Northwest, Eighth Edition._ University of Washington Press, Seattle and London.

Kirk, Donald R. 1970. _Wild Edible Plants of the Western United States._ Naturegraph Publishers, Healdsbury, CA.

Logsdon, Gene. _Successful Berry Growing._ Rodale Press, Emmaus, PA.

Natural History 9/93.

Norwood, Erika.

Organic Gardening, Sept./October, 1993.

Reidel, Jennifer. Interviewed, 1986.

Robertson, Laurel, 1976. _Laurel's Kitchen._ Nilgiri Press, Petaluma, CA.

Stapp, Dorothy. Interviewed, 1993.

Wild Berry Magic, 1982. Published by Paddlewheel Press, Tigard, OR. 97223